Sail Into Business

PAUL PETERS

sailintobusiness.com

Edited by David Zelnar

Copyright © 2024 Paul Peters

All rights reserved.

DEDICATION

For my loving and supportive parents
and my wife Tonya.

CONTENTS

Acknowledgments	1
Introduction	3
My Story	5
Getting Started	30
Business Structure	53
Marketing and Advertising	63
Proposals	73
Getting Paid	85
Watch For Scams	93
Success Stories	102

ACKNOWLEDGMENTS

I want to thank, first and foremost, God! My loving wife Tonya, my wonderful parents, Pete and Gwen, my son Clayton, my brothers Gregg, Michael, and Robert, my family, and my close friends who have always been there for me. I am thankful that I can help others, and most importantly, I am thankful for the people that have helped me. Over the years I have met so many special people through my business, church, and friends. I've always said, "I'm thankful for the people I've met, the people I know today, and the people I will meet in the future."

Sailing with Tonya in the Dominican Republic.

Photo by Misty Kabernagel.

INTRODUCTION

Being self-employed has its ups and downs, such as sailing. One day it can be great and beautiful. Some days are very calm, others very stormy. As with business you must constantly learn your trade, you never want to take anything for granted and especially with how things today change very rapidly.

The wind can be both with you and against you, learning how to navigate will get you home safely. Some learn these skills faster than others, but you can move at your pace. Business principles remain relativity the same for all types of business, big and small.

As with sailing you don't just buy the biggest boat first, you start out small, if mistakes are made, they are small and you can easily overcome them, as you get better you move on to a bigger boat. Both things have a lot in common as does starting and growing a business. Please note, I'm not an attorney or accountant but sharing what I have learned through practical experience.

Paul Peters

MY STORY

Every journey has a purpose,

You just have to find yours.

Family Picture.

I grew up in a middle-class home; my father had a respectable job with Western Electric (AT&T) and my mother worked for my family's local candy company Wockenfuss Candies. We were a family with four boys, me being the youngest. We all went in different directions, yet we all were determined to succeed on their own merits. All of us went to public schools, only I was able to go to a private high school, Calvert Hall College, not on my academics and not on my soccer playing ability, although at the time we were ranked consistently in the top 5 schools in the state of Maryland and I ended up playing all four years at school.

Growing up I was always in the slower classes not because I was a goof-off or didn't try, I just was. I was in remedial reading classes from fourth grade through college. I had to take a reading class in summer school to get into Calvert Hall. My freshman year I had to take two classes of summer school to stay in, and my sophomore year I had to do the same. I could have fallen back to a public school where it seemed to be easier but I didn't. I graduated from Calvert Hall in 1986 as one of the lowest in my class but thank God I made it through due to my determination of not wanting to fail.

Moving forward I got into Towson State University, now known as just Towson University, through what I call the back door, which was the College of Continuing Studies. This allowed me to enter Towson without a high GPA and SAT scores and after establishing a GPA of 2.0 I'd enter the university as a regular student, which I never did. Again, Towson required me to take a remedial reading class; it never seemed to end with reading. So, as with Calvert Hall, I was determined to not flunk out. During my freshman year at Towson, I took Pre Civil War History, thinking it was a subject that I liked and understood. Well, once again I started falling behind. So for one exam I studied, studied, and studied some more. I got 68 out of 70 on my multiple-choice quest-ions, great right? I had full -page answers to my three essay questions, I was so happy leaving that exam, at least a "B" I figured. Got the results back I got 68 out of 100, I got three zeros and failed. I was so depressed, not understanding why. My professor wrote me a note to come see him, probably because he was baffled himself. He told me that I had written a list of facts and did not examine what I read and define it. DING! DING! The bell went off, I couldn't comprehend what I read, I could only memorize facts. I have Dyslexia!

Me, during my younger years, on own Boston Whaler in Ocean City, Md.

I continued on at Towson taking any classes I could get into that were open and never getting my GPA up to a minimum 2.0. Years later I received a letter from Towson stating they did not wish for my return (as I say), but really I failed out. I still tried for another year going back to community college, but to no avail.

So what am I going to do with my life? I knew at a young age I wanted to become an entrepreneur but didn't know exactly what I wanted to do. I knew I was never going to be hired by a Fortune 500 company, I knew I always had a job at our family's candy company but I wanted to be my own boss. But what would I do?

Well, my oldest brother offered me a sales job with his franchise, Money Mailer. I took it, traveling almost an hour back and forth to the College Park area working for a year or so. Then I was offered a franchise to buy in York, PA. My parents loaned me some money and I was off being an entrepreneur. This gave me some of my pride back, I felt good about myself and I could go out with my college-graduated friends and not feel like an underachiever.

Well, that lasted about a year or so, and then I started working with my other brother Gregg on the weekends cleaning cars at people's homes to make beer money. I was able to sell Money Mailer and get out of that massive franchise agreement. It was a huge mistake buying that franchise. Could I have tried harder? Yes, but being young, I thought it was a good chance to take. Although I lost money and failed again, I learned a lot from the experience. Today, I understand failing is not a bad thing, if you're going to be in business you are going to fail.

At this point, I was working with Gregg, as he had started a home maintenance business. We started out cleaning cars, windows, gutters, decks, and so forth. Not being able or fair to Gregg, I never wanted to be his partner, he was already established, I started a parallel business working with him but keeping our finances separate and began to grow my own business. But the difference I made was getting my home improvement license and insurance which allowed me to get commercial jobs. Continuing to work with my brother, not against, and learning and sharing our combined knowledge we grew both of our businesses together.

Clayton on vacation in Hilton Head, South Carolina.

At first, my business name was Universal Home Service, but I did not incorporate it when I named it, not having the money to do so at the time. When I finally went to incorporate the name, someone had recently claimed it and incorporated it, so I had to come up with another name for my company. I wanted a general name that said what I did without having my personal name in it. So, Maintenance Required Inc. was formed. Slowly I grew my business with an old property truck that I had bought for $800. It was rusted, missing the tailgate, holes in the seat, view of the road through the floorboard, but it was still great. Gradually, I bought the equipment that I needed to move into painting as an added service that I provided.

I got married, and my wife at the time worked for a good company, GE Capital, so she was able to provide well-needed health insurance. We had our son, Clayton, in 1999. We had a good marriage and did the things that families do. But like my mom, I don't think she was ever happy with me being self-employed and not having a steady income coming in. But being stubborn, I continued building my company. Fortunately for me, when I had slow times, such as in the winter, we still had a paycheck coming in every week. So, around ten years after starting Maintenance Required, I began doing very well.

I wanted to expand with new businesses and invested in a start-up thinking I made it over the hurdle. I had extra money to spend, so I did, borrowing and spending tens of thousands of dollars. I purchased a new truck and better equipment, and invested more into our business, Waves of Color. Some of this money I never recovered and I never reaped the re-wards of some of my investments.

When everything in my life was rolling along in the early 2000s, my last business, Maintenance Required, was a contracting business specializing in home maintenance, painting, repairs, window cleaning, deck cleaning, staining, and much more. I was making more money than I ever had before, reaching a goal of gross sales that had eluded me up until that point. I started thinking of new ways to earn money offering other types of services to build my business even more. One way was buying a multi-media stripping machine that I could use in the off-season. In Maryland, it gets so cold that you can't do much outside work in the winter. In this new business, which I named Enviro-Blasting, I could strip boat bottoms of their old paint, mold remediation, fire restoration, and more. I had a new logo made and got a dot-com for my new name.

Then my brother was moving from Baltimore to the Delmarva Peninsula wanting to start a new painting and home maintenance business in the area where we spent our summers growing up. So we came up with a name for the business, Waves of Color, now Waves of Color Painting. I invested money into the start-up and the development of the name, logo, website, and advertising hoping again to fill the winter void of our off-season work in Baltimore. I was hoping to get into condominiums, doing inside paint-work for people in the off-season since it was a beachside area.

Waves Of Color advertisement.

Then came the idea of this business, unnamed at that point but now called Sail Into Business. I wanted to help new start-ups by using my knowledge of being in business for over fifteen years and helping people navigate through all of the trials and tribulations of the ups and downs of being self employed. Although none of my businesses failed, Waves of Color had a hard start due to what was to come, the crash of 2008. This put a lot of small businesses out of business, but my brother Gregg, who operates it completely today, has made it into a very successful company and it is well known in the area for its professionalism and ability to provide high-end service and timely completion of work.

Enviro-Blasting made me some money but again with the crash, it had to be put on the back burner, similar to my current business. We had to do what we did best just to survive. But I never lost the idea for my consulting business but just didn't have the time and money to devote to it.

I had this business idea, now my current endeavor, back then. I went into media blasting, helped start a new business in Delmarva, and spent money like I was going to make what I was making every year and counting on it. Well, the crash of 2008 hit, and caught every business off guard, a lot of businesses fail-ed. Moving forward, I had debt from loans I took out and had to survive. I put everything on hold other than my main business and did whatever I had to do to survive. Thankfully, I had a great customer base, even though they also cut back on the services they wanted from me. It took a couple of years, but I survived, I think it took its toll on my marriage, something that is common. So a divorce followed but I remained friends with my ex, agreeing to continue to raise our son as a team.

Tonya and I on a pier in Melbourne Beach, Florida.

A couple of years later, I met my current wife, Tonya. I was ready to move on, my goal was to make it successful in my business for thirty years and wait until my son graduated from Towson University and closing my company. (I still retain the name, logo, and con-tractor's license to operate in Maryland). I never had any lawsuits against me, not one worker's-comp claim, not one general liability claim, and not ever having a client not pay. Pretty decent for someone who had always struggled with learning. I just learned a different way and learned what my God-gifted talents are. I sold my house, and we moved to Charleston SC for a year. My plan was to only clean windows. Well, the business never got off the ground, so we decided to move again this time to Indialantic Beach, Florida, and again take up window cleaning for a small business for me, not having any employees, payroll, huge insurance bills, etc.

Another fifteen years passed and throughout the years I asked my clients, friends, and other business owners what they thought about my new business idea. I received positive feedback and added to my idea for this new business. I was getting tired of my business, Maintenance Required, and wanted to move on.

My goal was to finish with a successful thirty-year run of my business without having any lawsuits, any worker's compensation claims, any general liability claims, or unpaid invoices. I wanted to leave on top. I also wanted to get my son Clayton out of college. I didn't think it had any value, come to find out it did.

American Flag
Charleston, South Carolina

So Tonya and I lived in Charleston for about a year, it was nice, but was becoming very overcrowded. I started a new business, City and Surf Maintenance, primarily just doing handy-man jobs, window cleaning, and anything I could do by myself without any employees or the constant headache of payroll and insurance of multiple vehicles and employees.

We moved again, this time to Indialantic Beach, just outside of Melbourne, Florida. I continued City and Surf Maintenance in the new location, and like any new business, it took time to network, advertise, and market to start making money. This was supposed to only be a small business to make money and nothing more, using my knowledge to hopefully get up and running quickly but it still takes time. Most people think they can start a business and it will start making money right away, this is the farthest thing from the truth that it typically takes years to make a profit from a new business.

One day I was riding up the coast on a gorgeous afternoon and I thought to myself, "Paul, why don't you do what you have wanted to do for a long time?" Start a business that helps new businesses by educating them on basic business principles, what they might need, what mistakes one could make, motivational, inspirational, and development-al. There are a lot of people who don't go to college but might want to go into a trade business or have a wonderful skill they could use to make money. This could even be something for the college graduate who might not been taught practical business skills. People who grow up in a family business are fortunate to learn all of this while they are young, but some people don't have that experience. So that night I started putting everything together.

It's hard starting a business; my father once said that as you get older it gets even harder. First, you have to have an idea for your business and money that you are willing to invest and maybe lose. The business needs to be something that fills the void that other businesses don't provide, make it better (you don't have to reinvent the wheel) just find a better way of doing it, adding new ideas to your method of sales and marketing.

You have to make a business plan and a business model. You need to do your research and estimate how much money you'll need, what types of licenses and insurance you'll need, find a location, and so on. Even being as experienced as I am, I knew I had a lot to learn. For one, marketing is different today than it was thirty years ago, even though old-school marketing still works and should still be used today.

The first thing I had to do was come up with a name, but what kind of name? A name that isn't personal or reflective of my name. This is because if you want to sell your business, and you have Paul Peters Consulting as the name then you really can't create a brand name around it other than for yourself. How many people do you know that have talked about starting a business? Practically everyone. Writing a book about their life? Lots of people. It can be done. It's hard, a lot of failures will occur, unexpected issues, divorce, a big storm, COVID, the death of someone close, etc. I started brainstorming on a new business name, it took a long time for some reason, sometimes it can take days or weeks and maybe months. Then to come up with a name that nobody has is even harder. It hit me either that night or the next but in a very short time, the name Sail Into Business came to me.

Sailing is like business; some days are beautiful, some there isn't any wind, some there's too much wind. There are stormy days and days that start out great but end terribly bad. What a great theme, I love water, but who doesn't? But surely someone, especially living in Florida, would have that name, you would think right? So the first thing I did was go to my GoDaddy account and see if it was available as a dot-com, no way a dot-com would be available, surely someone already has it. Now if you don't know it's very hard to get a dot-com vs. a dot-net or dot-us and all the other dots that are out there now. To get a dot-com is truly rare today. And to my surprise it was available, I didn't think twice and bought it for thirteen bucks. Boom, all mine! Next, I started my outline for the business to tell people what I would be selling. Online services, email services, Zoom, in-person coaching, seminars, etc. I created a document with all I could offer a new start-up business in a PDF, including how much would I sell my service for.

Before and After Photos of a Fire Restoration and Painting job by my company Maintenance Required.

Next, I needed a logo, and I needed to register my name with the state of Florida for a tax ID number, again nobody in Florida had this name. I couldn't believe it. I needed to figure out what my logo was going to look like. I'm not an artist so I needed outside help.

I was working with Keith Schachter, who owns B2K12 Branding Solutions in Melbourne, Florida, for my other small business. I told him about my idea when we first met about a month earlier, but I was concentrating on City and Surf Maintenance. I called Keith, who already knew of my idea, and I told him I wanted to move forward with the development of Sail into Business. Keith loved the name and Googled it while we were talking. He said the name is great but someone already owned that dot-com, I said I know, that person is me! I don't think he believed it but it was true. So Keith and his team started developing a logo, gave me a couple of samples and I picked the one I liked the most. Then, I needed to start building a website and getting business cards printed. Yes, you still need business cards. There's a new trend of having business cards on your phone to scan but I think physical cards are still better, so you should have both. I knew in the beginning that my business was all about marketing so I would need to spend most of my money on just that. I didn't need much more other than a new computer and a new phone number.

Well, what are we going to put on my website sailintobusiness.com? He told me that I needed someone who could write my outline so I could sell it, but he wasn't available to do it.

Docks done by Maintenance Required.

He told me, "You should have your outline writen professionally." I said OK and he gave me the name of a published author that he thought could help me. So I called David Zelnar, who is currently living and writing in Tanzania, we talked and David suggested, "What about a book?" I said, "A book? Never in my wildest dreams thought about writing a book, but why not!" So here you have it.

Completed Home Painting and Staining.

Finally, I needed professional marketing and coaching. I met Brandan Payne of Payne Point Media. Together we have produced professional studio commercials that will air on my social media platforms; Facebook, Instagram, LinkedIn, and others to come. I joined the local chambers of commerce and Toastmasters to improve my public speaking. All of this in only two months.

This is something I have wanted to do for years, putting my experience and talents to work so I can help others. Everyone can help, you can volunteer, donate blood, clothes, food your time, or money. There are so many things you can do the help others. People who give, wish for nothing in return. They want you to pass it on to another cause. I had many obstacles growing up as we all do but you have to keep moving forward and learn from your mistakes and failures.

Completed Home Painting.

Completed Bathroom Remodel.

Thank God for everything he has given you. See the silver lining, always taking something good out of every situation or problem you might have. Be thankful, you didn't get here alone; many people have helped you along the way. Believe in yourself when others might not, don't give up on your dreams. Take that first step, even though it's hard. Learn to pivot, listen to others' advice, and avoid naysayers. Life is short, so make it good, and address your problems and fears headon. Try something new and different.

Being self-employed is hard work, it's risky, and takes a lot of failures with a lot of trial and error, but if successful it can be extremely re-warding. The story is to be continued. Follow your dreams and take act-ion. Your original plan will change, you have to learn how to pivot and adapt, always tweaking things in your business while always understanding that business principles don't change. Don't be afraid to look for and ask for help, and remember you get what you pay for. Surround yourself with great people and great things will happen. You just to have trust your idea while also being careful of the bottom feeders out there trying to take advantage of new businesses.

Painted Bedroom.

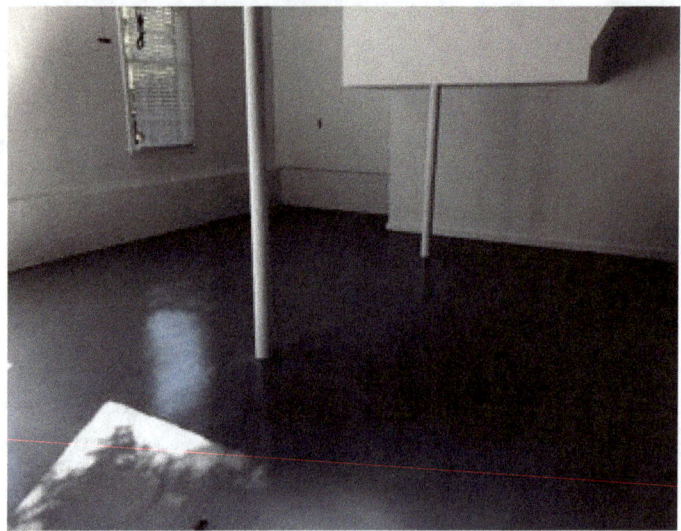

Painted Garage.

There are a lot of good people who will offer their help to you, you just have to look for them and ask a lot of questions, always double-checking on everything. You have to get your hands dirty, and you can't learn everything from Google or YouTube, even though these are good aids. Join networking groups or trade groups where people share their information for free. Be careful if you are successful to not grow too fast. Unknowns are always just around the corner. Go at your own pace. This book is a guide to help you navigate through your new business. May you have the best of fortune in your new endeavor.

GETTING STARTED

Many people have great ideas,

But successful people have a plan.

So you want to be your own boss and start a business. You have an idea, skill, or product that you believe is marketable and can be successful. But you're setting sail into the waters of business for the first time. If you want to keep your ship afloat, then you need to be prepared for whatever the sea may throw at you.

This section will go over everything that a new company will need in order to be legitimate and successful. From making a business plan to the minor details many first-time business owners overlook. It is important to be prepared and begin day one on the right foot. One shouldn't leave shore without first setting a course.

Make A Business Plan

Many people start a business without a plan, thinking they can just wing it and the business idea is good enough to keep the company afloat. This couldn't be farther from the truth. Running a successful business means being prepared for obstacles that may come your way. Before you quit your day job and pursue the life of self-employment you need to crunch the numbers. Start by adding up all of the costs that go into a job or product. Make sure to include fuel, labor, parts, rent, utilities, and every other expenditure no matter how small; some may seem minimal, but I promise the little expenses add up. Now figure out the price of a typical job, service, or product. How many jobs or products do you need to sell to break even and how many do you need to cover your living expenses? Now that you have your goals and know what you need to do or to make to stay afloat. Constantly keep updating this chart and monitor your expenses and profits. This will keep you on track and will let you know if you are in a position to grow or need to cut back. I suggest making a ledger with simple T-Chart or create Excel Sheet. Here are some examples.

COST	CHARGE
JOB 1 $$$	$$$$$
JOB 2 $	$$$
TOTAL	TOTAL
$$$$	$$$$$$$$

Job	Equip.	Fuel	Ttl. Cost	Charge	Profit
1	$$$	$$	$$$$$	$$$$$$$$	$$$
2	$$	$	$$$	$$$$$	$$
Total	$$$$$	$$$	$$$$$$$$$	$$$$$$$$	$$$$$

Now that you can visualize what you need to succeed, you can start setting future goals. I.e. "If I can consistently get x amount of jobs, then I can expand or purchase a new vehicle or accomplish whatever your next goal may be. I find it helpful to make goals based on 1,3,5. One month, three months, five months or one year, three years, five years. Having a short-term goal gives you an instant sense of accomplishment. Having reachable, short-length goals gives you realistic steps towards achieving your long-term goal.

Start-up Capital

Having a good business idea is great, but to put your plan into action you need to have some start-up capital. Businesses consistently have unexpected expenses and you need to be prepared so that an unforeseen cost doesn't derail your company.

Saving enough money ahead of starting your business could be difficult and could take a long time. There are options to get the money that you need if your current income or savings isn't enough to supplement your business expenditures.

You can take a small business loan from a bank or credit union. There are several programs and opportunities out there for small businesses to get their start-up capital. Having a business plan already drawn up gives you an advantage in your presentation to these lenders.

You could also find an investor or business partner. If you don't want to go to a bank for your start-up capital or get denied, a private investment might be your best option. Of course you might not know someone who is able to invest large sums into your company. There are investment groups and meetings that allow new companies to pitch their business ideas to people with capital to spend. There is more information on the different types of business structures later in this book.

Don't quit your job until established.

Business Name

The name of your business is crucial and is the first thing that customers will know about your company. It needs to be unique, catchy, and easy to remember. Coca-Cola wouldn't be as popular if they were called John's Soda Company.

You also need to think of the future and one day being able to sell your business. Many people want to put their name in the business, but this makes the business seem small and unable to handle larger accounts. It also gives it very low resale value. Paul Peters Painting doesn't have a large market if I decided to sell the business to pursue another venture or retire. Few people want to buy a business that they have to rename and rebrand and rarely will they want to have a business named after someone else.

It's best to have a versatile company name. Something that isn't so specific. Business changes and you don't want to trap yourself in a box if you start offering other services or decide to pivot your company's focus. If I own Paul Peters Painting and start offering landscaping services,

I don't want to have to consistently tell potential clients that we do landscaping too. The landscaping could end up being our better service, but our name makes it look secondary or nonexistent. If my company name is Home Upgrades, I am not limited to a single service, even if in the beginning that is all that I offer. I have given myself room to grow and I have a name that is good for resale, including my domain.

Business Account

One should always separate their business finances and their personal finances. The best way to do that is to open a separate account for your business. Any money that goes into this account is for business purposes and expenses. Pretend that you and you as a business owner are two separate people. You earn your paycheck from the business, but its balance doesn't belong to you. So many times, I've seen business owners use their company credit and debit cards for personal things, bills, or meals. They always promise that they'll reimburse the company or that it's ok because business is good. But these erratic purchases can be a killer for a business, especially a new one. The business can only stay alive if it has capital. If the business is turning a large profit, feel free to give yourself a raise if that increase is consistent. If it's just a spike from a big job, offer yourself a small commission and save the rest for added security for unexpected business expenditures, down periods, or paying off business debt. Keep track of all purchases that you make with the business account and save your receipts. Make a spreadsheet on Excel or a similar program. You can also make a simple T-Chart of expenses and earnings. This will allow you to see where the money is going as well as where it is coming from. This way you can monitor what expenses are cutting into your profit the most and adjust accordingly. If your boat is taking on water, this will allow you to find the source.

Get Licensed and Registered

Certain municipalities and states require a business to get licensed before being able to open. This is especially true for contractors and food vendors. Most licenses are quite easy to obtain and only require filling out a bit of paperwork and paying a fee. This is also true for registering your business, but depends on the type of company.

You will probably need a federal tax ID number, also known as an Employer Identification Number (EIN). It is free to apply for your EIN. You may also need to get a state ID business number, but this is dependent on which state you are opening your business and that state's income tax laws. The process is usually similar to the federal. Tax ID numbers allow the business to pay state and federal taxes, which you want to be up to date on. The last thing you want is to lose everything because you were not current with your taxes.

Liability Insurance

I know that adding an additional expense like insurance may seem like something you can put off until you are more established, but liability insurance really is a low-cost safety blanket that you should have from the moment you open.

Depending on the type of business you are starting, you may have to get other types of insurances as well like Workers' Compensation and Commercial Auto. You should look up what kinds of insurances are required by your state and local municipalities for your industry. It is always better to be prepared for a situation, than to find out that you needed a certain type of insurance and have to shut down until you have it or worse get sued because something happened and you didn't.

Computer and Printer

This one may seem like a no brainer, but I have seen plenty of business owners try and run their company strictly on their phone. You need to have a functioning computer, with your traditional office apps like Excel. If you are able to purchase a computer that is just for work, I would suggest you do so. That way you can keep your business and personal life and files separate.

In the modern age so much business is done via the computer. Invoices and contracts are sent typically sent electronically, although it is a good idea to print and keep a hard copy just in case. Spreadsheets, client lists, and other important business information is best kept on a computer and not stored in a phone or only available in hard copy.

Website

One of the most important things you can have for your business is a website. It makes your company look legitimate and increases your chances of being found online. It's important to include your company name in the domain and to make your name as simple as possible so that it's easy to remember. When you go to register your domain, this will also let you know if your company name is unique and if you need to change it to help you stand out.

It's also a good idea to have a .com instead of the other options like .org, .us, and .xyz. These other domains may be cheaper and are more readily available, but having a .com makes your business look more professional and successful.

Now you may not know how to make a website, but there are several websites that can walk you through the process like Wix and GoDaddy. Your website doesn't need to be complex, it just needs to look professional, function properly, and be accessible.

Email

Your email address should reflect your company name. Many times I have seen people give out their personal email which not only looks unprofessional but it's also best to keep your personal and business correspondence separate so that you aren't sifting through private emails looking for one from a client.

The best email address to have is info or your name before your domain.

For example:

info@sailintobusiness.com
paul@sailintobusiness.com

These kinds of email addresses do cost money and if that is an issue when starting your business there are other options that are free.

For example:

sailintobusiness@gmail.com

Phone Number

Having a consistent and unchanging phone number, as a business, is extremely important. Clients need to be able to get in touch with you and having to find out what your new number is could deter them from using your company and might even imply to them that you are out of business.

If possible, have a business number that is not your personal line. Not only does this make your company look more professional, but it also separates your business from your personal life. When the business line rings, you will be conditioned to answer as the business. It's always a good idea to answer with your company's name, "Thank you for calling ____, how may I help you?" It may seem simple, but this legitimizes you as a serious business.

Business Cards

Business cards are an essential tool for networking and for giving potential clients a physical reminder to contact your company. They are something that you should carry on your person at all times because you never know who you are going to meet and where that introduction will happen. The last thing that you want is to not be prepared when you meet a potential client or someone that could be important to your business.

Exchanging numbers is an option in the absence of business cards, but contacts can be forgotten or lost, but a physical reminder is still the best bet. It's also a good idea to have a virtual business card in case you don't have physical ones available. These are a good way to share your contact card and are easily downloaded to your phone as a QR code.

Equipment/Supplies

Before you can start taking clients, you need to make sure that your business is well equipped to get the job done, and done properly. Now, it's important to start small and get what is necessary and buy everything for the business you see in the future. The last thing you want to do is go in the hole for equipment that you never or rarely use because isn't needed to do the work for the clientele you have or are getting. Get the necessities you need to run effectively and buy as you go or as it's needed. Set calendar and income goals for purchasing upgrades and new equipment. Expand as you grow, so that while you are getting your name out there, you aren't looking at a massive debt that deters you from your vision. The first year of owning a business is already hard enough without this added financial pressure of succeeding.

Work Vehicle

A reliable vehicle is a key piece of equipment that every business owner should have, especially if you work in the service or contracting industry. Having your car break down, preventing you from being able to complete jobs is not only an income killer and an added expense, but it gives the customer the impression that you are small and not up to the task. I know it can happen, but if your vehicle consistently needs repair and is in horrible shape, then it may be time to invest in a new one. Now, I'm not saying go out and buy a brand new vehicle, have it wrapped, and then start finding clients. But having a dependable and presentable work vehicle not only gives your client a good impression of your business, but it guarantees that you are able to do the job and your transport is an asset and not a liability.

Proper Attire

The first thing a client is going to notice is how you or your employees are dressed. It is always important to present yourself and your employees to them as professionals. If your business is in an office, then you and your employees should be in business attire. If your company is in the trade industry, then your employees should be wearing uniforms, or at the very least be wearing t-shirts with your company logo. A uniform not only shows professionalism and makes your employees look like part of a well-oiled machine, it also puts into the minds of your employees that when they are wearing it they are representing the company. Subconsciously they will be on their best behavior while wearing a uniform, because even if they are not on the clock, poor actions while in uniform could cost them their job.

Professionalism

The way you present yourself and the way your employees conduct themselves is how your client perceives you. When meeting a client, always dress appropriately and be well groomed. This is typically their first impress-ion of you and your company. You should keep all aspects of your business organized including paperwork, tools, and any other work related items and workspaces.

Your manner of speech should also be monitored and professional. Don't curse or use slang around the customer. Don't bring up controversial topics. Don't make crude jokes. You can be friendly but remember that this person is your customer, not your buddy. And if you are working at the customer's home, mind you p's and q's even if they are away. Many homes have cameras and you better bet that they are going to be watching them.

If you're listening to music while doing a job for a customer, make sure that it isn't explicit. Don't have it at a high volume and only use one ear bud so you can hear your client if they need you.

Always turn off your music while talking to a customer.

Don't smoke on the job, this includes vaping. If it's a long job and you really need to, make sure you are out of sight and don't take too long or too many. Customers notice if you're consistently gone on smoke breaks. And it shouldn't have to be said, but no drugs or alcohol while you're working.

If you are a business owner, you should also be mindful of what you post on your social media. People will look you up, especially if you are working inside of their home or business. Don't let a post be the reason why you are losing clients. You are the face of your business so what you do or say, represents your entire company. Be mindful of what you put out there or make public. You can also make posts that only your friends can see, so that you have additional privacy.

Paul Peters

BUSINESS STRUCTURE

Not all businesses are the same.

There are several different types of business structures and you should weigh the pros and cons of each before deciding which is best for you company. Most small businesses start as a sole proprietorship, partnership, or LLC and eventually if they get large enough they "go public" and become a corporation. This sect-ion will give you insight into the different business structure options that are out there for you to determine which is how you should structure your business.

Sole Proprietorship

A sole proprietorship is an unincorporated business that is owned by a single person. One benefit of having this type of business structure is that it is easy to start and all of the income and deductions will show on your personal tax return. You are automatically considered a sole proprietorship if you do business activities and aren't registered as any other type of business.

There are downfalls though. Sole proprietorships do not produce a separate business entity, so your business and personal assets are not separated. Sole proprietorships also do not have limited liability which means you can be held personally liable for debts and obligations that the business has incurred. It is also difficult to raise funds, as there is no stock to sell and banks are more hesitant to lend to sole proprietorships. This type of business is good for low risk businesses and for people who want to test their business idea before forming a more formal company.

Partnership

A Partnership is a business or firm owned and ran by two or more people. Having partners can ease the burden of start-up costs and labor. But a major issue with having a partnership is that you and your partner(s) must agree on issues. You may also find that your partner is not contributing as much as you are which is not only frustrating but can be hard to rectify since the company is in both of your names. In a partner-ship you are responsible for decisions that your partner makes without you. You can also be responsible for them if they don't pay their taxes. If you start a business with a partner, you need to make sure that this is a person that you can trust and is not only reliable but is responsible as well. I personally would not suggest this type of business.

There are types of partnerships that give the partners some reassurance. Limited partner-ships have one general partner with unlimited liability and all of the other partners have limited liability. The partners with limited liability tend to also have limited control over the company, but that depends on the partnership agreement. Profits are passed through to personal tax returns and the general partner must also pay self-employment taxes.

Then there are limited liability partnerships, which give limited liability to every owner. This type of partnership protects each partner from debts against the partnership and keeps them from being responsible for the actions of the other partners.

LLC

A Limited Liability Corporation or LLC is a business structure where the members are not personally liable for company lawsuits or debts. A LLC is taxed on a "pass-through" basis. All of the profits and losses are filed through the owners' personal tax return. But with an LLC, you are protected from personal liability in most instances and your personal assets aren't at risk in case the LLC faces bankruptcy or lawsuits. Profits and losses can pass through your personal income without you having to pay corporate taxes, but members of an LLC are considered self-employed and must pay self-employment taxes towards Medicare and Social Security.

You don't need a board to create an LLC and can be created for a sole proprietorship or partnership. LLCs can have a limited life in many states and when membership changes, someone leaves or joins, some states require the LLC to be dissolved and reformed with the new membership unless there is a preexisting agreement within the LLC concerning buying, selling, and transferring ownership.

LLCs are great for owners who have significant personal assets that they want to protect, and who want to pay a lower tax rate than they would with a corporation.

Corporation

A corporation, also known as a C corp, is a legal entity that is separate from its owners. Corporations offer the highest protection for its owners because they can make a profit, be taxed, and can be held legally liable separate from its owners. All business related expenses can be deducted including gas, insurance, internet, mechanical issues with your vehicle, advertising, bookkeeping and accounting fees, licenses, interest on bills, loans, and rentals.

It does cost more to form a corporation than other business structures. Corporations also require more extensive record keeping, operational processes, and reporting. Corporations pay income tax on their profits and sometimes are taxed again when dividends are paid to shareholders on their personal tax returns.

Corporations have an advantage when it comes to raising capital because they can sell stocks to raise funds. They can also use stock options to entice employees. Unlike an LLC, when a shareholder buys or sells their stake in the company, a corporation can continue to do business without having to restructure. This is the best option for businesses that plan to "go public" or be sold in the future.

S Corporation

An S Corporation or S corp is a special type of corporation that is designed to avoid the double taxation of C corps. S corps allow profits and some losses to go directly through the owners' personal income without having to be subject to corporate tax rates. Not all states recognize or tax S corps equally although most recognize them the same way that the federal government does. S corps have to qualify and be registered with the IRS, speak with an agent to find out if your business is eligible for S corp status.

Paul Peters

MARKETING
&
ADVERTISING

People can't buy from you,

if they don't know who you are.

One mistake I have seen many small businesses make is not advertising. They think that their company is so amazing that people will just come to them and they can rely on referrals and "word of mouth". And sure, if you do an amazing job, you might get a client to tell a friend or two and one may even hire your company. But that is not going to help your business grow and limits your companies reach to just people who know people you know. That circle can only go so far. No matter how big your company is you need to draw customers, and the best way to do that is to advertise and network. Here are some of the best ways to get your business recognized.

Join Local Business Groups

There are several local networking groups that you can join. They are easy to find and only require a simple Internet search. These groups can be helpful in finding people in your industry that can help you grow your business and make connections that you otherwise wouldn't have. Sometimes it's not just what you know, but it's who you know that gets you past your current threshold. Most business groups do require a member-ship fee, so make sure that the group or groups that you are joining are beneficial. If you're a tradesman, it might not be useful to be in a medical networking group.

Join Local Chambers Of Commerce

Chambers of Commerce are a great tool for your business to network and find new potential clients. Membership fees tend to be low cost and are worth the spend to have your name on the registry. Many new residents will check their local chamber to find the services that they require. If your business works in several chamber jurisdictions, it's wise to join as many as you can.

Print Ads

One of the best ways to reach potential clients is through local print ads. There are a variety of options that are directly sent to customers like mailers, local magazines, and coupon books. Mailers are a good way to get a promotion out to a targeted area, but also run the risk of going straight into the recycling without a second look. Local magazines are a good way to target homeowners in your area, as they tend to be the most likely recipients of these. Coupon books are a great tool to drive in new customers, but the clientele that tend to use these can be one-stop customers who are only interested in the single deal. Signs around town are another great way to get your name out there, but you need to be wary of local restrictions so that they aren't taken down. Signs at local stadiums, ballparks, and schools are perfect if your company's target customers are parents or kids. If you really want to show your area that you are the company to go to, a billboard makes sure that you get noticed.

Digital Ads

The world has gone digital and so should your company. You can target clients using Geo-location through Google and other platforms. These targeted ads are great to keep you top of mind for clients. Make sure that when you go digital in your advertising that you focus on narrow sectors and service areas near your business. Build local business and then expand. You don't want to stretch your business too far taking jobs that are a great distance from your base. If your business does something that can be shipped or done digitally then digital ads can help you reach a much larger audience outside of your area.

Social Media

Just as every person seems to have social media accounts these days, so do businesses. Social media is a great tool to reach potential customers and to show off your work. Every company should at least have a Facebook page, an Instagram account, and be listed on LinkedIn. Your business should be posting once or twice daily. The more active the accounts are, the more likely that they are going to be found. You should boost promotional posts at least once a week and invest in Geotargeted ads for your business on all of the social media platforms you currently have for your business.

Charitable Marketing

One of the best ways to promote a business as a staple of the community is to show that the company cares. There are so many ways that your business can give back and market itself at the same time. Sponsoring a Little League team is a great way to show parents that you support their kids. If there are causes that are near to you personally, be a sponsor for their events. Your company name is typically mentioned at the event and on their site leading up to it. When potential customers see that your business cares about the same thing that they do, they feel compelled to give your company a chance.

Diversify Your Marketing And Build A Brand

You know the old saying, "Don't put all of your eggs in the same basket." The same can be said for your advertising portfolio. Diversify as much as possible. The goal of marketing isn't always to get the customer to call right away, it's having your company be the first one they think of when they need a service you provide or at the very least have your company be recognizable when they make that Google search. The more a customer sees your logo, the more likely they are going to pick your company. Repetition brings comfort and gives your business the allure of stability and recognition.

PROPOSALS

Make sure the price you're charging, covers your costs.

One of the most important things a company should do is be concise with their estimations. Customers want to know where their money is going and don't want to be surprised by poor estimates and unexpected costs. This section will go over all of the things that you should consider and prepare for when making an estimate for a client.

Make A Written Estimate

When giving a customer an estimate you need to make sure that it is written and you have a copy for invoicing. Do not write your estimate on the back of your business card or a scrap piece of paper. You can give one by text, but I wouldn't recommend it. It is best to give an estimate via email or on some sort of form that you can copy and use for your own records. Giving the customer a proper written estimate gives them the security of knowing what their money is going to and alleviates any bargaining tactics that they may try to use to get a lower price. Have your customers confirm that they received the estimate to avoid any future excuses of not knowing prices beforehand. You can even use the estimate as a contract by just having both parties sign and date the document. Make sure that your estimates are simple and clear as to what services you are providing. Do not charge for an estimate, most companies don't and it makes you seem cheap. Stick to your estimate, even if you underestimated the job. It's fine to let the customer know that your costs were more than the estimate but don't charge them the difference, take it as a lesson. If a customer asks you to do extra work that isn't on the estimate, explain the time and material needed and add it to the estimate so that there isn't any confusion.

Have Estimates, Invoices, And Client Information On File For Reference

One thing business owners should do is keep track of their clients, business expenses, and profits. There are a variety of tools that you can use that can keep this information in order like a CRM or Excel Worksheet. You should also have a paper filing system and your digital files backed up to the Cloud just in case. You should get a customer's full name, address, and email to keep on file. This is not only a good way to organize your clients alphabetically, but it's also good source for sending mailers and email blasts about new products or promotions. You should look up clients so that you make sure that you are dealing with the business owner and that you have the correct spelling. I always have the customer personally write or send me their email so that I know that it is correct. Whenever you finish a job, compare the final costs to your estimate. Take notes of what needs to be adjusted and apply it to your next estimate.

Compare Prices With Competitors

You should always be aware of what the average market price for your service is and what your local competitors are charging. You don't want to be the cheapest option out there, but you also don't want to be losing clients because you are the most expensive. You want to be fair but profitable. Check around and see what other companies are charging and base your prices on what seems right.

How Valuable Is Your Time?

When making an estimate, you need to ask yourself, "How much is my time worth?" If you were working for someone else, how much would you be asking for a salary or by the hour? Now this doesn't mean think of your dream number and add that to the bill, you need to be reasonable with your estimates. But don't take on a job that you know is not worth your time. And, also don't tell a customer that a job will be finished in a week, when you know that it will probably take longer even without any unexpected issues. It's best to give a range in your estimate and not tie yourself to an unrealistic date. This makes your company look more reliable and doesn't inflate the bill with labor costs that are far beyond what was quoted.

Compare Every Estimate With Costs

Every time you purchase something that is in an estimate, make sure to compare the costs. Prices of material can fluctuate and having the most precise information at hand can help prevent you from undercharging for items and losing profit. This includes if your service requires fuel costs to be included in the bill.

Don't Cut Costs Just To Increase Profit

People will check to see if something looks overpriced. Don't let customers feel like they are being scammed because you think that they don't know how much something costs so therefore you can charge them anything and they won't know the difference. They will and word will get out that your business isn't to be trusted. Now if you're customer thinks that your prices are too high, you can offer a cheaper material to lower cost, but be upfront with your customer about the quality and never use a cheaper product just to save money without their consent. Also, don't let the customer try and provide the material for you. As a business you are probably going to get a better rate and you know exactly what you need, whereas the customer probably doesn't. It also makes your business look small time if the customer is only using you for labor and doesn't trust you to provide the supplies.

Work In Costs To Upgrade Equipment Or Get New Equipment Needed

Your goal in business should be to consistently expand. It is alright to add in a small miscellaneous charge that is designated to purchasing a new piece of equipment that you need and will use often. This can help you get to owning the equipment faster. If there is a piece of equipment that you need for a single job or a job that you don't do often, rent it don't buy. You can also work into the estimate or final bill a shop charge for items that you might need to replace after a job, for example a good paintbrush.

Keep Prices Consistent

What you charge one customer should be consistent with what you charge every customer. Don't give discounts because someone is your friend or a member of your family. Never charge based on what you think a customer can afford. People talk and you can quickly ruin your reputation because you charged more to a wealthy client for the same job that you did for a person with a lower income. Don't give referral discounts, people will already refer you if you did a good job, but they will also share with people if you didn't. Make sure to be fair to yourself in your pricing and don't go too cheap because you are just starting out and looking for customers. The customers that you have may be repeat clients and it's difficult to raise rates when someone is accustomed to what you have been charging. If you do have to raise costs, you can always offer a free ad-on service for loyal customers.

GET PAID

Show me the money!!!

Now it's time to discuss the whole reason why you started your business in the first place, to get paid. This section will not only go over different ways to get paid for your services but will also review other issues when it comes to income. One might think that it should be easy, I do a service and then I get paid for that service, but there are lots of other things to consider like deposits and how you are tracking your billing. Not every client is going to be the same and not every payment is going to be the same, so you need to be prepared.

Forms Of Payment

Cash is always king. It's guaranteed, you don't have to pay any additional fees on it, it's of instant use, and it's legal as long as you report it. You can offer cash discounts for your clients to help you reduce your transaction fees, but that is entirely your decision on whether it is worth it. But you also don't want to be running around town with a suitcase full of money especially if you're doing bigger jobs that cost a significant amount. Plus most customers aren't willing to pay for expensive services in cash, if they even carry any at all. The world has moved to cards over paper and your business needs to be equipped to accept all major credit cards. You will have to pay a fee of about 2.5-3% for each transaction from the credit card companies, but you can add this to the customer's bill. It's not uncommon to do so. The last thing that you want is to lose a customer because you can't accept their form of payment. You should also accept digital transactions from aps like Zelle, Venmo, Pay-Pal, and CashApp. The more ways a customer can pay you, the more you can guarantee that you get paid.

Deposits

Taking a deposit to secure business or help cover upfront costs for a job but do not make the deposit too large. It should not be more than twenty percent for small jobs and large jobs you can have the client pay in thirds. If you are taking on a job that you can't afford to pay the upfront costs, even with the deposit, bring in another company to help you cover part of the job. It's better to do the work well and share the profit rather than try to attempt something that can overwhelm your company and cause it more damage than good.

Having a client put a small deposit on a future job is a good way to secure that future venture. It gives them the security that they have guaranteed your service for that time and it lets you know that a client is serious about having the work done. It is up to you if you make these deposits refundable. I would suggest doing so unless you have had to spend an absorbent amount of time preparing for a job that was then cancelled.

Billing

When billing a customer you should be thorough and list all expenses and fees. You should have a simple contract between you and the client. You can use your written estimate as a contract if you have both of your names, amount, along with tentative and completion dates. Each job should have an estimate and a final bill, which should be matching as close as possible. If you take personal checks, try to get paid at the end of the service, so that you don't have to wait until it comes in the mail or have to continually contact the client to collect.

If you are giving a repeating service, such as cleaning, lawn care, or accounting you should bill on a monthly or bimonthly basis.

Commercial Vs. Private

Your business may have commercial and/or private clients. Payment structure tends to differ between them. Corporate jobs tend to pay with a mailed check on a biweekly or monthly basis, whereas private jobs typically pay immediately upon completion of the service. Commercial jobs tend to be bigger and therefore worth the wait, but if your company can't afford to go without payment after finishing a job, then it's probably best that you wait to take on this type of work until it can. You do not want to overwhelm your company in pursuit of grand profits if you are not ready. You must conquer the bay before you can cross the ocean. Don't worry, there will be other commercial clients available when you are ready.

Plan For Offseason

Some businesses are seasonal or have a time of year where business goes stagnant. This is especially true for companies that are dependent on the weather like pool cleaning or on necessity like tax prep. If you know that there is a time of year where your workflow is going to decrease, you need to be prepared. Set aside money for these off months so that you can make sure to cover payroll and other essential expenses when profits are down. You should also come up with a service that you can offer in the slow times that can help keep the ship afloat and keep the amount of water taken aboard to a minimum. Having poor cash flow can sink a business, having a plan to keep the income stream steady can be a lifeboat.

WATCH FOR SCAMS

Not every client is honest.

My business journey was not always perfect. Sometimes you have a customer who seems trustworthy, but in the end is just trying to scam you for add-ons and free services. I had to learn the hard way, so I wanted to share a couple of examples of the few times that this happened to me. Luckily I learned my lesson and how to recognize if I'm being swindled or not, so this rarely happened. Hopefully these examples will help you avoid having these situations happen to you first hand.

One time I got hustled was when I got a lead from my friend's company for a repaint on a big old mansion north of Baltimore. I gave the customer an itemized estimate for the work that he was looking to have done. He chose to have the majority of the work done then and to wait for the other work to be done at a later date. The estimate was $35,000, he came back to me on the estimate and said, "If I pay you $30,000 upfront will you take it?" I would never recommend doing this, but I accepted. We proceeded to start our work on what was agreed upon in writing. This was a big job for me at the time, the largest single sale I had made at that point in my business.

Well, then the hustle started. First, he told me, "Well, while you're here, can you paint my outside mahogany furniture?", I said, "Sure, but that's not included, I will bill you for time and material." He responded,, "Then aren't you going to strip and paint the back door area?" No stripping was not includeed. Then he asked, "When are you going to start painting the dormers?" There were twenty of them, three stories high. I told him, "That was itemized in your original estimate and you chose not to have them done at this point and it would cost another $15,000. It went on, but remember I was paid in full.

He thought he could use his legal knowledge to trap me. I produced all of the paperwork; everything I said I was going to do and had completed. I had one job left that I estimated, painting the inside stone in the cellar, this was an old mansion and did not have modern basements like we have in Maryland. The basement was about another $3,500. I had finished everything except the basement at this point, which included the add-ons that the customer added. I had had enough, I figured out his game and walked away.

Later, I got a call while I was coming back from Baltimore. It was 105 degrees outside, and my truck was overheating, so I pulled over and talked to him. He insisted that I meet with him in person to discuss everything; I said no, everything was completed. I told him that I was finished and that's when the threats started, but I held my ground.

Come to find out he was one of the largest land property owners in Baltimore. He would snatch up property from the poor who failed to pay their land rent (there is a law in Baltimore City that if you own the home you still have to pay land rent). This guy was a scumbag. I looked him up and there must have been over 100 lawsuits that were placed against him.

Some people try to charm you in the beginning, knowing all along they think they are smarter than you and will try to use that to get extras. I never heard from him again.

Here is another example. I gave an estimate for two small interior jobs, I estimated them separately but wanted to do them at the same time and gave a discount if they did them simultaneously. I did the job and was paid. Then the gentlemen asked me to come back on a Sunday (I usually don't work on Sundays unless it's an emergency). But I did and painted his girl's bathroom. Once completed, I gave him the bill, which was itemized. I billed him the full price without the multi-job discount. He argued that because they were done in the same timeframe he should get the discount. We could have easily painted the bathroom saving on setup, cleanup, and travel when we did the other rooms. I ended up giving in and granting the discount even though the job cost me more to do. He got me.

One thing you have to be careful of is somebody stealing, either from you or your business or if you have a business that goes into people's homes or other personal spaces. Unfortunately, stealing occurs. How you deal with it will help you from having a problem or being accused of something can make a huge difference. People might take things thinking they might not be missed be-cause you thought of them as a trusting person or you think the person who is working for you is trustworthy. There are all types of stealing many of them are categorized as petty theft. The closest people you trust can steal from you, friends, family members, partners, and anyone else you can think of.

Some things I worry about at night or not at my workplace are someone making a false claim on your workmen's compensation, stealing food from your workplace, taking home a small tool off of your job site, paying for their food or gas on the company credit card, and so on.

When I worked in people's homes, I always told them to put their valuables away, and never to leave money, jewelry, or important documents out. Some people would leave cash out to see if it was there when they returned as a test. One story I heard was about a nanny who was taking one piece of Sterling silver eating utensil home every week or so, thinking that the homeowner wouldn't notice or that it might have been someone else who did it.

Beware of every opportunity that could be a scam. If someone accuses you or one of your employees of stealing, tell the customer that you would be more than happy to call the police and file a report. Some people will do this to not have to pay you what you are owed. The good old flimflam can happen to the unexpected new employee, you need to tell them to remain calm and call a manager.

Here are some other common examples. Two people are working together; one brings attention to them by making a scene while the other is lifting something from the shelf. One of your employees allows a friend to take something for free or is charging them way less than what the sticker price is. Excepting a cash tip for something that an employee might have done extra for a client. Doing a side job for a friend using the company tools and equipment to work for someone else.

One time when I was working to start up our new business on the Delmarva Peninsula, my brother had a lawsuit against one of his customers who failed to pay him. When we first set up the business it was not a partnership, but at the time we had equal investment in the start-up of Waves and Colors, almost eleven thousand each. We each had separate bank accounts and just kept a ledger on who spent what and we would make things equal at the end of every month. Gregg's client countersued him and only because we had a photo together for an advertisement, they added me to the suit. I explained to the court, that we operated like a franchise, which we were individually insured and had separate bank accounts, but they added me because at the time I had more assets. Well, the judge ruled in my brother's favor but it cost me time, money, frustration, and worry.

I was working for a very good client who I never had any problems with. She said her neighbor needed some quick power washing done for a party. So I dropped everything and went over to her house on a weekend to help her get her pool deck and furniture cleaned. I handed her the bill, and she said my husband pays the bills and that he will send you a check. It wasn't for that much money but weeks passed and I had to send out two invoices. I finally got paid, but the woman wasn't spending her allowance money, and she clearly had wanted her husband to pay me. The lesson is to make sure you make a contract/agreement with the one who is paying the bills. This can work both ways. You can even look up who is on the title of a home.

In all businesses, people will use you for your knowledge, business license, professional status, etc. Be careful, they might be doing this to compare prices to use your paperwork to get something taken off of another sale such as a settlement of a home. All sorts of ways people can use you only for just the paperwork stealing your time and effort. People might accept your price feeling that they are being overcharged but they think they are smarter than you and they will work you for every last penny or continue to ask for more things to be done without being charged. You can always do a little extra as good will but draw a line. People might try to dodge paying you by making all kinds of excuses, be clear about when you will be finishing and have your invoice ready a couple of days in advance and present it to the customer leaving a spot on your bill to add additional expenses/labor if needed. If a person is slow to pay you in the beginning this is what's called a red flag! They will be slow to pay you at the end.

Paul Peters

SUCCESS STORIES

Learn from those who took sail before you.

Sometimes hearing how others overcame their obstacles and succeeded can inspire you to do the same. In this section I have compiled success stories from personal friends, colleagues, and my own triumphs in business. These will show you that with the right mindset, determination, and business acumen, success is just over the next wave.

Controlled Demolition Inc.

Controlled Demolition Inc. or CDI specializes in the implosion of buildings and mass structures. Founded by Mr. John Loizeaux Sr. in 1947, who first started felling trees and using small amounts of explosives to split large tree stumps to facilitate pulling the pieces out of the ground. He then gradually moved into using explosives to fall industrial structures. As the company grew, it became a full family business with Jack's eldest son Mark joining him and soon after his younger son, Doug, took a roll in the company as well. Mark and Doug eventually took over the company and continued to build CDI into a global business.

CDI currently holds over eight Guinness World Records for the implosion of several different record-sized projects. I'm sure you have seen their work. They also had a niche in blasting buildings and structures for many movies. They were eventually able to trademark the word that defined what they did, "Implosion". The Art of Implosion has been used around the world. In the Movie, Enemy of The State, CDI used pyrotechnics to display a huge fireball as the building was imploded. Their work has aired on Nat Geo, The Discovery Channel, and The Learning Channel to name a few. Some structures you may be familiar with are the Seattle Kingdome, several Cape Canaveral launch sites, the Alfred P. Murrah Oklahoma Federal Building that was bombed, most of the retired Casinos in Las Vegas, and most recently in Brevard, Florida, the condo building that sank and partially collapsed. CDI has also imploded retired power plants in Florida and the UK.

The thing I most remember about the Loizeaux' was their character and professional-ism. They did things right. They did what they were contracted to do. And I did the same for them in every job they hired me to do.

This goes to show that if you have a vision, patience, and time you can grow your own business. You will have ups and downs, successes and failures but will need to learn from them and constantly adapt to what is needed.

CDI Bridge. Photo by Joe Grant.

Mark Koski

Mark Koski was one of my closest childhood friends. I met Mark in 7th grade, as we lived in the same neighborhood. We walked to school together every day and were in the church choir together, but we didn't play the same sports.

Mark's household was a little different from mine, I had three siblings living in a three bedroom house, but Mark was one of six kids in the same sized home. His father worked for the Postal service and had multiple part time jobs to support his family. His mother raised the kids until she could go back to work as a dental hygienist. Entering 8th grade Mark had intended to continue his undergraduate academic career at Calvert Hall College High School like me, but when he was offered a scholarship to McDonogh School he decided to go there instead. McDonogh School is a prestigious private school in the Baltimore area. After graduating from McDonogh with good grades, Mark moved on to a college scholarship. He attended Hampden Sydney College in Virginia, the third oldest college in the United States.

Mark Koski and I eating steamed crabs at my house in 9th grade.

After graduating with a degree in mathematics and a minor in economics in four years, he passed on becoming an actuary to accept a job with the company he worked with for the previous six summers. He accepted an offer from GYC Builders, Inc. back in the D.C./ Baltimore area. GYC is a custom home company building truly high-end custom homes. Gary Clark, the then owner, took Mark under his wing and taught him every-thing he needed to know about building a home from the ground up. Mark learned quickly and after five short years Gary made him a partner in the company. Six years after Mark became a partner, Gary Clark retired and sold the business to him. Mark said, "I started with nothing? I started with less than nothing! I graduated from college with nothing but debt." Mark continued to grow his business through hard work, gaining the respect of top business owners in the area and built a great reputation for providing high quality beautiful homes. Mark was fortunate enough to work for some of the wealthiest people in the Baltimore/DC area. Surviving the 2008 crash and benefitting from mutually beneficial friendships he developed through his business, Mark was able to diversify his investments and eventually began investing in commercial real estate. Mark eventually bought a shopping center with his long time friend, Gregg Bell, along the way.

Mark is an example of someone who took his athletic talent, along with his educational opportunities, and started, as he said, with less than nothing. What a wonderful friend; he has a great large family that supported him through it all, and Mark managed to remain humble as he continued to succeed.

Mark Koski's largest home to date.

The Wockenfuss Candy Company

My Great Uncle and Godfather, Herman Wockenfuss, who I affectionately called Uncle Dinky, started a small candy company in Baltimore, Maryland in 1947 after World War II. All he had at the time was a small candy stand in one of the old city markets in Baltimore. Moving from hard candies and licorice products to making home made chocolates. He would work in his basement at home making candy at night and on the weekends for the market store. Then he and my Great Aunt Marian opened a storefront on Belair Road from the basement of their home. Slowly growing, he bought a house two doors down from theirs and moved his storefront down the street, which gave him more room to manufacture even more chocolate products. Understanding the need to keep the business busy, because the candy business is seasonal, he decided to open a location on the boardwalk in Ocean City, Maryland in

1970. This location is still on 1st Street and has become a must stop for vacationers who visit every summer and has been operating for 55 years.

When I was younger, my great uncle told me to ride my bike down the boardwalk and give out some of their now famous pink candy shopping bags. This filled the slow time for his business, allowing him to keep his Baltimore staff employed year round. Growing, he convinced his son Paul Wockenfuss, who is the current owner with his wife Lynn, to quit his state police job and join him. My Uncle Richard Koch became the head candy maker. My mother, Gwendolyn Peters, became the manager of their new location at the North Plaza Mall located in Parkville, Maryland. Herman, or as we called him, "Dinky" provided jobs for many of us in the family. I started out scrubbing floors on my hands and knees, helped make chocolate rabbits for Easter, and assisted in other candy making.

I was able to manage stores at a young age, learning and being taught how to do things right. You name it, I pretty much did it. It gave me a great foundation of learning how a small business operates. I moved on to create a thirty-year successful business in part due to what I was taught working for the candy company and most importantly because I was taught how to do things right.

Making candied apples.

I have so many memories of working for the company over my younger years. One time my Uncle Dinky told me to ride my bike up and down the boardwalk a give out their now famous pink candy shopping bags. He did something different at the time and made his new location and business stand out from everyone else.

Here's a funny story from when I worked at the candy store. I was at one of the locations making a candy delivery and my great uncle still worked everyday and was working at this particular location when this woman walked in. She had a complaint about her chocolate Brazil nuts, explaining that the nuts were stale. So my uncle looked at the half eaten box, not just one or two eaten, but half of the box. He explained that he knows that the nuts were fresh; unknowingly to the customer she was talking to the owner, which he never disclosed. He said, "I'll refund your money or give you a new box of chocolates for free." He ended with a smile when he told her that he would make sure the owner knows of this problem. In business, the customer is always right.

I was over his and my aunt Marian's house doing work one day, and I told my uncle about this business idea I had. The business idea was this business, "Sail Into Business". He thought it was a good idea and offered me start-up money, I said no Uncle Dinky, I wasn't here to ask for money, I was just asking if you thought it was a good idea. Fortunately, I didn't take the loan because two years later in 2008, the market crashed. I had to do everything I could to keep my main business afloat and I dropped all of the other things I was working on.

Today the candy company is over 100 years old, still family owned and managed with 6 locations, moved into selling candy through in store kiosks and mail orders to all over the country. It's a true Baltimore icon.

Paul Peters

The Bryn Mawr School

I started working as a sub-contractor cleaning windows for an elite private girls' school in Baltimore, "The Bryn Mawr School" in 1993. At this school, there were two facilities offices, maintenance and janitorial. After being sub-contracted for a few years, the company that I worked for lost their contract. I was asked by the Head of the janitorial staff to stay on cleaning windows, so I did knowing it wasn't my company's fault that the contract was lost from the parent company that was subbing me out. I continued to clean windows on a campus of twenty or so buildings ranging from being built in the 1800s to recently.

I knew who was in charge of the maintenance and I wanted to get in on some of the work that they had that I knew I could do. Eventually, Bob, the head of facilities allowed me to estimate the campus gutter cleaning twice a year for over eighteen buildings on campus. Trust me it was not the best job to get, but it paid well and got me in the door to the facilities side. A couple of years passed and I started asking if I could write some painting estimates, saying I could do the first small job for free. I talked with Bob about other people and companies I had worked for and he finally gave me the opportunity to do a small painting project.

Well twenty-five years later, I not only did the gutter and window cleaning, but I ended up having most of the painting projects. I don't know an exact figure but after thirty years of service, I probably grossed well over two million dollars in work. This goes to show you that patience and persistence work. Year after year, always producing quality, on time, emergency, and consistent pricing. This school always filled my summer schedule, but I did not take it for granted. And Bob provided me with a great reference for all other jobs to come including a $250,000 job for staining and painting a whole townhome community.

Before and After Photos of the Bryn Mawr School Gym.

Before and After Photos of the Bryn Mawr School Auditorium.

The William Scotsman Corporate Headquarters Building

Once again I started working for The Williams Scotsman Company cleaning windows as a subcontractor and once again the company who was subcontracting me to them lost their contract but I was asked to stay on. So I cleaned windows for years and started to ask about giving an estimate for painting the whole building. It took about ten years before I was finally given the opportunity to bid on the job. I got it! $58,000 job! It looked great in the end; it was a great showcase because it was right on I-95 north of Baltimore for everyone to see. Again showing diligence in my work year after year and finely was rewarded with a great contract.

Me and my truck in front of the William Scotsman Corporate Headquarters Building in White Marsh, Maryland that we painted and cleaned the windows.

Payne Point Media

Brandan Payne started out like a lot of us, not really knowing what he wanted to do, dibble dabbling in different small jobs while he was young. His video/ photography passion started in high school and turned into him working with a radio station and then working at nightclubs taking pictures and videos. He wanted a business that suited his lifestyle, but he had to pay the bills. So he worked for Dominos as a driver, moved up to manager, and was able to attend corporate seminars, which taught him about structure. He went back to photography, working for Sears, and after exceeding the goals set by the studio, he was promoted once again and started volunteering to go to other locations to help out. Unfortunately, Sears went out of business, but he continued his and started a small studio in his garage. He learned how to hustle to get work (because that's what you have to do when you start a new business). Later, he picked up an internship with a big magazine company in New York City, The Source. He eventually got hired full-time to do their photographing at local high-end bars hosting celebrities. Then, he worked for a Mercedes Fashion Show, building his knowledge in photography. Well, then the unexpected happened, Hurricane Sandy, which caused normal business to change immediately, so Brandan had to pivot. This is something that you always have to be prepared for, the unexpected. Taking on more jobs over the years and continuing to learn about all types of businesses finally led him to start a full-time company, Payne Point Media, which he currently operated in the Melbourne, Florida area and is looking for the next new trend, such as AI marketing.

Thank you for reading my book, I hope this helps you while you set sail on your journey into owning your own business. If you are looking for more information, check out my website sailintobusiness.com and come to one of my seminars. My goal is to help you and your company embark on this business venture with the tools and knowledge to succeed. The waters of commerce can be treacherous, so let Sail Into Business be your compass to guide you to your self-employment goals.

Sail Into Business

www.ingramcontent.com/pod-product-compliance
Lightning Source LLC
Chambersburg PA
CBHW071832210526
45479CB00001B/108